T0208835

A MINER'S FAMILY LIFE

Memories of Minden, West Virginia

BILLY RAY BIBB

authorHOUSE®

AuthorHouse™
1663 Liberty Drive
Bloomington, IN 47403
www.authorhouse.com
Phone: 1 (800) 839-8640

Published by AuthorHouse 02/26/2019

ISBN: 978-1-7283-0084-9 (sc)
ISBN: 978-1-7283-0082-5 (hc)
ISBN: 978-1-7283-0083-2 (e)

Library of Congress Control Number: 2019901954

I dedicate this book and all the memories it contains to my family and the friends I had growing up in Minden, West Virginia.

I would like to pay tribute to my sister Sharon K. Barker for her time and assistance in preparation of the manuscript for this book. Many thanks, Sis.

I dedicate it as well to all the miners and their families who experienced life in coal-mining towns; I include every soul lost due to the primitive coal-mining processes they worked under that caused them to suffer in mind, body, and soul.

CONTENTS

INTRODUCTION

The stories I present here are not based on substantial facts or published records; they are my memories of a lifetime as a son of a coal miner and what I had heard from parents, neighbors, and friends in Minden, West Virginia.

CHAPTER 1

THE BEGINNING

When my mother was young, she would take her daddy's dinner bucket to the Rock Lick mine at lunchtime. Her dad was responsible for the mules and ponies that pulled coal cars out of the mine. She walked from her family's home in Concho, West Virginia, through the woods to get to the mine.

One day, she had trouble and lost her way, which made lunch late. The experience weakened her, and she contracted rheumatic fever, which left her with a heart murmur. She was not aware of this until she was nearly forty-seven, when regulating her blood pressure became a problem. She eventually died of it.

Mom and Dad married in 1935. Their first home was just a washhouse they rented from a miner who was able to rent a house. Because not all miners could rent homes, some had to rent rooms in boarding houses the coal company owned. When those rooms were all rented, people would have to get on a waiting list.

Dad went to school through third grade, when he was about the age and size to start his mining career. I think he started out in the mine on the coal belt sorting coal and slate. Many young boys got their start in that manner. He was one of seven sons, and his dad was a miner too; it was a family custom. Dad was able to read and write.

Mom ultimately received a bit more education; she graduated from grammar school. We always asked her for help with homework, especially math. She was great with math; she could figure problems out in her head but not on paper. She made us work hard in school, and I guess we did all right because most of us finished eighth grade, some graduated from high school, and one attended college. Some attained more education on the job or in the military.

I do not know how Mom did all she accomplished. She was a stay-at-home mom who raised eight children. Later, she worked when my older siblings were able watch the younger ones. She was a cook at Minden Elementary School for a while, and she cooked as well at the Chuck Wagon Restaurant. When the old doctor's office became a nursing home, she cooked there and helped the nurses' aides. I think at some time that she worked at the Oak Hill Hospital with food and nursing.

I would like to include our family tree here, but so far, I do not believe it has bloomed. Some members of our family have conducted genealogical research for a number of years, but last I heard, they were undecided whether there were any Native Americans among our ancestors. In my childhood, I was told that my maternal great-grandmother was a full-blooded Native American. It would help this story a lot if I could actually come up with evidence of that.

The best I could find out about my paternal grandfather was that he received a different last name, one given to him by a family he lived with. I know little more than that, but I consider it interesting.

When my parents' names came up on the waiting list, we moved to our first home, a two-room house on Arbuckle Creek in Minden across from the post office and company store. It was the second house down from the Minden Community Center and what used to be the Methodist church. This occurred when our family included three children.

One young couple we lived near could not find a place to rent, so they cleaned out the chicken house at their parents' home and worked endlessly to find and fix up furniture. Once they finished, we saw red curtains hanging on each side of the one little window that had no glass. They had worked very hard to make a home in which they could start their lives together.

The next house we lived in was the third house on the right side of the road at Scrappers Corner; it was a three-room house where three children were born. Nowadays, it's in very bad condition on an overgrown lot with weeds and with trees all around. The roof is falling in on the back room. The area it is in was in a flood zone, but family members never talked about its being flooded in those days, the early forties. My other brother and sister were born there also. We were eight all together—my mother, my father, my five siblings, and me. Then we moved out of Minden.

Dad managed to get a house on Salem Road next to the building housing the coal company's power supply and air blower. It was across from the meatpacking house. By that time, I was five and my younger sister was four. Mom seemed to like that home better.

Those were hard times for the unemployed and homeless. During the Depression, sometimes, a knock at the door would herald someone asking for a handout. One day, a man came by, and Mom sat him at the kitchen table and prepared a meal for him. He was very grateful and went on his way. That was the first home in which we had a gas stove. The cheese sandwiches Mom toasted in the oven were great on winter days.

We got our first brand-new television set there; it was green, and it sat on a rollaway table. And the box it came in was just the right size for us children to crawl in; we had some fun times with that. That was the beginning of our watching TV Westerns.

Several times, cows would get loose from the meatpacking plant. One day while we were playing in the yard, a number of them came down the hill and filled our yard. We fled as if our lives depended on it, and we hid under the house; we were scared silly as you can imagine.

This was the first house we lived in that had a well; hauling water was a new experience for us. We had a large garden in which we grew a lot of food to eat and preserve. We had many chickens as well. Mom would often prepare chicken for dinner. Someone would have to kill one by cutting off its head with an axe. It would flop around and try to walk without its head, and blood would fly everywhere. After a time, my mother started wringing their necks two at a time and say, "See? No blood." We also raised hogs for meat in a pen back in the woods.

One time, my older brothers were throwing rocks into an apple tree to knock apples down. My job was to collect what fell, but one time, a falling rock gashed my head. Someone picked me up and put a cloth to my head. We went in my dad's old pickup truck to the doctor in Minden. I still have a large scar on the top of my head caused by that piece of red dog, which is rock left over from the coal extraction process; the highway department used it as gravel. Red dog drew heat from the sun and burned all the time.

During our last year or so in Salem, my tonsils were taken out. I spent thirty days in the Oak Hill Hospital and received thirty shots of penicillin, and I failed first grade because of my extended absence. The next year, my younger sister and I were in first grade together; we attended a two-room schoolhouse on a hill on the road to Concho.

We moved back to Minden from Salem to a house on Daisy Hill, past Minden on Arbuckle Creek just beyond a railroad crossing.

I remember a man performing a trick with two quarters he held in one hand and got them to click against each other, which we kids loved.

If you continued on Daisy Hill beyond the railroad crossing and Dog Hollow, a sharp right turn would take you up a curved hill, Daisy Hill itself. We lived in our house there, on top on the left, for several years. Dog Hollow was a single-lane road on which a good number of coal company houses were. Houses were built in rows, some on the sides of Minden Road and some in alternating rows on every hill. There were names for all those hills such as Number 1, Number 2, Storehouse Hill, and Schoolhouse Hill. Now, lots of road numbers and names have changed due to satellite imaging of maps and roads in GPS grids. A bit of homemade Mountain Dew, let's call it, was rumored to have come from some of those hollows.

The family grew again on Daisy Hill; another sister was born. We came walking home from school one day and found that Mom was in a terrible way. She sent us to a neighbor's house to ask her to call the ambulance and then come to help her. We did not know quite what to do other than what they told us. We spent time with our neighbor until the rest of the family came home. Soon, we had a new sister—eight kids, Mom, and Dad living in a four-room house.

We didn't live in that Daisy Hill house for long, but we did spend many hours listening to the old radio and our little TV. Apparently, that was a time smack dab in the middle or beginning of cowboy days. The old-time country and cowboy music songs I listened to on the radio affected my mind to a great degree. The sound of whip-poor-wills gave me a lonely, faraway feeling, and the cowboy songs prompted me to imagine living on the prairie, carrying a gun, and all the rest of that way of life though I was not very old then.

Listening to guitar music prompted me to make one out of a cigar box, a long, narrow board, and some rubber bands as strings. I loved to strum on that thing and sing at the top of my lungs—what joy. And I would swing on an old rope swing under the front porch, which was tall and allowed me to swing very high. That was the atmosphere I enjoyed on Daisy Hill.

In winter, I listened to songs about Christmas. We kids would mentally prepare ourselves for Christmas Eve and Santa's coming. We'd wonder when we would hear Santa's sleigh bells. Snowy winter days provided us with some but very little excitement, but watching the snow turn black was amazing.

A steam locomotive would chug up the hill from Thurmond pulling a very long line of empty coal cars; its wheels would spin on the cold steel rails and send sparks flying like lightning. That was an exciting sight to see at night from a front window of our house on Daisy Hill.

That was not the last time we moved; we left and then returned to Minden a number of times. The houses we lived in were rough; they were all made of wooden boards with cracks, and that made those places hard to love. We usually had to paper all the walls with heavy wallpaper to keep the cold air out and then paper over that to make those places presentable. The houses had running water and electricity but no hot water or heat other than fireplaces and kitchen stoves. The bathroom—a privy—was way up on the hill. It was painted white with black trim, and no one could miss seeing it in all its pride and glory.

CHAPTER 2

EXCITING AND
CHALLENGING TIMES

I mentioned something about homemade Mountain Dew some time back, and that reminded me of a poem I wrote.

> Way down there, I wondered
> and stumbled very far.
> I met this sweet ol' honey
> coming with a jar.
> I said, "Chase me down the mountain
> and throw me in the creek,
> For my bladder feels like a melon and I
> have to take a leak."

I have been sitting on a stump
all day sipping from a jar.
I feel like I am still sitting there,
for I have not traveled very far.
This wide mouth was full this
morning of my Mountain Dew,
But now it looks very empty, or
maybe this jar has just turned blue.
I can't see anything in it—or is
that one last drop of dew?
Whew!

An uncle's neighbor and his family of many children lived in Dog Hollow. Their mule died one day, and they buried it in their small front yard. I recall that the whole family would ride in the back of an old pickup truck in and out of Dog Hollow with their long hair blowing in the wind.

We later moved to a place called Harlem Heights and lived in a coal company house. The company's electrical and fan house was there; it pumped air into the Minden mine. A superintendent usually occupied these homes in Salem and Harlem Heights and operated the powerhouse. I guess Dad had some favor with the company real estate person to acquire use of the two homes. The Harlem Heights home was way off the hard road on a large, winding, red-dog road, and the other place was nearby.

We had to walk down to the hard road to catch the school bus and back up after school. Our oldest brother would ride all us kids in an old pickup to the bus stop on bad winter days. I was pretty small and short. I was able to lie in the back window on top of the seats while everyone else crowded in the front seat.

We three smaller kids would run around there in the summer wearing little and having lots of fun. We'd get on an old tire swing and have our older siblings push us as high as we could go.

I remember enjoying Mom's biscuits with thick slices of tomatoes on them. We had a large garden that included a grape arbor. One day when I was walking, I saw a large copperhead snake slithering near my bare feet. I did not waste any time leaving the scene.

Our house was a company house that was similar to other houses in Minden, but it had plaster ceilings and walls, so we had less to do to keep the cold air out.

One day, some company carpenters came to the Salem house to plaster the ceilings and paint some rooms.

It was not very long until we moved again to a house in Gatewood; we called it the swamp house because it was near a swamp. We got water in buckets from a spring behind the house. That place wasn't as good as the last two places we lived; it had cardboard on the walls, and we did not live there long. Mom was not going to put up with that.

I recall Granddaddy Murphy riding his old mule from Minden over the hill to visit us in Gatewood. Our brothers and I would get up early to build a fire in the wood-burning kitchen stove and make coffee, which had the best flavor from having been brewed on that wood stove. Our oldest sister began dating there; her boyfriend would come with milk and cookies for us kids, and we had fun hiding from him behind the couch. We were very bashful kids, you know, back in those days.

Our house was near a cemetery on the hill. A whole family had been wiped out by the black plague. Our stay at Gatewood was not very long. We moved back to Minden and lived in a house on the hill above the carpenter shop on the right side of the hill.

CHAPTER 3

A MINER AT REST AND
A LUMP OF COAL

Back to the Harlem Heights house—I recall Dad working the night shift there, so we kids had to be quiet or play outside when he was trying to sleep during the day. I know that was a daunting task for Mom after a while.

We would watch our old TV before bedtime, and Dad would get up, turn the TV off, and take the cord with him, so we'd have to go to bed when we were too noisy. One night, we were watching an old Boris Karloff movie that was very scary. When it was over, the girls had to go to the toilet outside in the dark a ways out from our house. I took the opportunity to spook them; I hollered, "Here comes Boris Karloff!"

and they started screaming! That brought Dad out of his bed. Well, he grabbed me and whipped me with his belt he used in the mines. It was very heavy leather and very strong. After losing what I thought was my last breath, I cried for a very long time. I can tell you I never did that again.

The next morning on his way to work, he found me playing outside. I guess he was very sorry for what he had done because he gave me an oatmeal cake from his lunch bucket. I do not recall what he said, but I was not interested in conversation, so he just went to work.

We lived on the right side of the hill above the carpenter shop for a while, and the next thing I knew, we moved to the left side of the hill into the last house there. Dad had some knowledge about a punch mine at the end of the road on the right side of the hill where we moved.

Not long after we moved, the company granted Dad some rights to dig some coal in the hill below our house to compensate for a hole in the ground that mine operations had created on our property. Dad and two older boys mined coal from there for a while to sell in the community, and I recall helping some. We would dig thirteen wheelbarrows of coal to make a ton that we sold I think for $8. A neighbor who lived in the last house on the right side of the hill very near where we mined the coal would drink and get a little talkative every once in a while and shout out occasionally. I believe he did not like us using the road in front of his house to haul coal.

We mined that coal until the dirt overhead in the mine became unstable and threatened to create more holes on the surface. Mom said we had to stop. That was the end of our family coal-mining company.

I feel my dad must have had had a good relationship with the coal company's real estate broker. As a matter of fact, I played with his younger son, and an older brother was good friends with the older son.

We were able to move in and out of Minden, the coal-mining camp, to two houses outside Minden. Salem and Harlem Heights were company houses. Gatewood was not. It was a private property we rented.

CHAPTER 4

FUN AND FAMILY

My friend and I rode bikes all over Minden, Rock Lick, East End, and the main town of Oak Hill. On Saturdays, we would ride all day, but on school days, we had to stay in the yard unless we received permission to leave it.

Sometimes, I went to church on Sundays with friends. My brother and I would go to the city dump in Concho to shoot rats with a friend's .22 rifle. We did not have any guns; Dad spread the rumor in town that he had a shotgun, but I believe he did that just to protect the family; I never saw it.

One Sunday, we had company from Kentucky—our uncle, who was Mom's brother, and his wife, our aunt. They came around lunchtime, and Mom offered them lunch though she didn't have anything.

She grabbed me and asked me to ride to the market for lunchmeat, and I was very happy to do so because I loved to ride. Can you image being vivacious and strong enough to be able to do that these days? I went and got back as soon as I could, and we all had lunch.

While we were living in that house, we helped Dad build a cellar in which we planned to store the vegetables we grew. We also built a garage on the hill beside the road. The land was so hilly that Dad had to build up the hillside to make a level place for the garage. He used trees he chopped down for poles for the garage, and he sided and roofed it with used rough boards and tarpaper. There was no place to store tools and equipment there, only Dad's old Dodge truck.

We raised a large garden there, and we cleared a plot to plant corn. The ground was yellow clay and very rough to plant and grow a crop, but we used a lot of 10-10-10 fertilizer. We also witnessed our first hog killing. We killed one of our two hogs for meat. Dad had Grandpa Murphy come, shoot the hog, and butcher it. I had never seen so much meat. We were still young kids. We canned many quart jars of beans, corn, tomatoes, and fruit of all kinds especially blackberries.

Every year from then on, we kids picked as many gallons of blackberries as we could to satisfy Mom's desire to can usually about a hundred quarts. After that, we picked more that we sold to everyone in the coal-mining camp.

After our family coal-mining adventure played out, we moved for the last time. Dad made his last real estate deal with the coal company; he bought four houses on the hill at the right side of the railroad crossing in Minden. The house on the left at the railroad crossing was where my dad and his family had lived when they were kids; he was one of seven boys and three girls. His dad, Grandpa Bibb, worked in the mines just as my dad did for twenty-five years. Several of the boys worked in the mines until they went to war or until the mine closed. One uncle who served in the war had stepped on a mine that blew half his foot off. Most of them moved to Ohio for work in the factories and retired there.

CHAPTER 5

GROWING UP

Back to the last move—Dad's intentions for buying those four houses were to live in one, renovate and rent out another, and tear down the other two, which we did. He, my brothers, and I pulled off every board and removed every nail, which we sold for lumber and other building supplies. When two of my our older brothers were drafted, Dad and I finished the houses. We planted gardens on the plots of the two houses we tore down.

I would call on many homes in the area to sell the vegetables—cabbage and tomatoes included. One of our neighbors was the butcher in the company store until it closed. In its last days, a company employee was running the store. After that, someone from Oak Hill bought the entire stock and sold everything until it was all gone. A friend and I were hired to work part time cleaning up the place, dumping trash, and doing anything else he needed help with.

I ran across a small electric jigsaw in the stock room, and I made a deal to work it off helping in the store. That tool allowed me to pursue my hobby—making various model wagons using wooden fruit crates that were there—grape, orange, apple, and so on. The wood ranged from a quarter-inch to three-quarters of an inch thick, and the thicker wood worked well for the wagon floors while I used the thinner wood to make the more intricate sidepieces and wheels. I must have made twenty or so wagons including a covered wagon, a rickshaw, a fire wagon, a farm wagon, and several more of different kinds. I entered them in a craft fair at the high school I attended in the sixties.

The freight elevator in the stock room the store was electric and was operated by pull cables—one to go up and the other to go down. It was old, but it worked well although slowly. One time while we were coming down from the upper floor, we pulled on the stop cable, but it responded rather slowly. That allowed the elevator car to go down below the bottom floor, and we found ourselves standing in a foot or so of water.

One summer, Dad came up with a $2 scrip book that the coal-mining company used. He told us to go to the company store for some ice cream. It was a warm summer day, and we wound up with a big glass bowl to put it in. It was a good ways from our house up above the hill where the Ripolls had lived. Several of us barefooted kids walked down the road and mountain path past the carpenter shop and a deputy sheriff's house by the big office building next to the store. We spent the whole $2 of scrip on vanilla ice cream; they put it in the big bowl. As we climbed back up the hill on the way home, all our eyes were on those scoops of melting ice cream. By the time we got home, the ice cream was floating around in the bowl.

When winter came, the garden plot was the perfect hill for sledding. We had an old sled, but others improvised by using anything slick that would slide down the hill as we screamed and laughed for joy.

One of my poems tells more about our family life then.

Life in a Coal-Mining Town

This life in a coal-mining town,
You just could not let it get you down.
Life each day was brighter
on the other hill,
Where the sun shined at will.

Winter brought snow about every day.
On our side of the hill, it seemed
it would never go away.
It was an awesome sight to see.
What joy it would bring for me and
some entertainment for the whole
family.

Complete change of winter joy
Brought to each little girl and boy.
Up and down that slick hill we would
go until we couldn't feel our toes.
But the wonderful, white morning snow
later turned very black you know.

In that day, it was the way to be.
This all happened so naturally.
That black snow because of the mine,
Coal dust each day seemed like it would
never melt and go away.

It was somewhat funny how
the sun only would shine,
On one hill, not the other, all the time.
There was no delighting it,
We were a coal-mining town.

Poem:

We were a coal-miner family,
We lived in a coal-mining town.
We lived in a town called Minden,
Where men mined coal from the ground.

A creek ran through Minden to the
New River toward Thurmond Town.
West Virginia is coal-mining country
where men dig coal from the ground.

I dedicate this short, down-
to-earth poem to the miners
who undercut the coal,
Who drilled hole to place dynamite,
Who hid as best they
could from the blast.
Who shoveled the lumps of coal.

Having a tiny light upon their heads.
Through the air they breathed
polluted to the point of zero vision,
Wanting to make sense of it all
to provide for the family.

Something just eats at me when I write my poems. I want to express the feelings, the fear, the responsibility, the nobility of coal mining—digging every day at death's door and not actually knowing if it is real. Will it open today to another world? Not any slave labor here? No underground existence? No more terrible blasts to survive? No more black dust to breathe that may send me to an agonizing death and no breath?

There is nothing as agonizing as feeling your breathing is restricted. Imagine your hand over your mouth and nose. Now separate one finger and breathe in the smallest amount of air you can. Imagine this amount of air gradually slowing down to next to no air until you cannot breathe anymore.

Dad had black lung, siliceous, and emphysema, so he had hard time breathing. Sometimes, he would hold his chest and try to breathe deeply, but he could never breathe deeply enough. How many people living in coal-mining towns have come down with these same diseases? One person who stayed home every day as a homemaker died of siliceous. She lived between the railroad on the front side of her house, sidetracks, and the main line to Thurmond. The hard road was in front of her house, and there were two train tracks behind her house. The space between these was only a few feet from her company house. Imagine people who didn't work in the mines but were still exposed to its harm. I suppose mining conditions have improved; God knows I hope so. But as for the safety and air quality there, I still wonder.

CHAPTER 6

SCHOOL DAYS

We moved to a house at the railroad crossing and a trestle. My younger sister and I attended fourth grade together at Minden Elementary. Our teacher was Mrs. Rapp, a very stern and tall person whom I feared. She was very nice and pleasant but direct and firm in her teaching methods.

The teacher I admired most was Mrs. Morton, whom I had for sixth grade; she made learning interesting and fun. She too could be stern and direct, but she would smile pleasantly most of the time. She liked music also; she always had the class sing together. One day, she asked my sister and me to sing together, and she said she loved the way we harmonized. We were pleased to hear that and enjoyed singing for her.

She especially liked the way we sung "Beneath the Lemon Tree."

The next year brought more science study. Mrs. Elva James taught seventh grade, and that was the first year we had a science fair. Another student and I entered an all-electric dollhouse we had made out of scrap wood—four rooms, two up and two down and all lit up with supplies Pop Williams, the principal, provided us from the school's supplies. I made a small wooden TV set for our house with a picture of John Kennedy, the president, that was lit from behind. Our house also had an elevator that ran from the first to the second floor thanks to John Crone, who lent me his Erector set motor. We won first prize that year. A picture of our dollhouse made it into the *Fayette Tribune* with an announcement of the science fair. That experience prompted my interest in combining woodworking, mechanics, and electricity.

The next year, we had our first male teacher. I believe the girls in the class thought that was interesting, but the boys didn't share that feeling because he was very handy with Mr. Williams's wooden paddle that resided in the furnace room. It was a long plywood paddle with half-inch holes in it, and it was very effective, or so I was told. I never was subjected to a paddling because I had a dad who early in my life had taught me to behave.

We lived close enough to school that we went home for lunch. That could be good or bad depending on what time of the month it was. The food available at that time was not very great; I remember going home for a bowl of rice for lunch.

By that time, the mine was closing. Dad's lung condition was finally diagnosed, and we had very little income then. He won a case against the coal company for black lung and was put on disability, and things got better when he became eligible for Social Security Disability benefits.

By that time, two older brothers had been drafted or had joined the military, and they helped the family some. Our oldest sister had married and had moved away, and two more sisters were nearly engaged and would be leaving home soon. My younger sister and I were going to high school the next year.

Very quickly, our first year of high school gave us an idea of how much or how little we had learned in grade school. Every class was a mountain we had to climb. My sister did better than I did. She was a little brighter I guess. I failed ninth-grade English the first half-semester, and I barely passed my other classes.

In tenth grade, I was directed to vocational training. Once I completed classes in reading blueprints and welding, I felt I had found my niche; my grades improved greatly. In eleventh and twelfth grades, I was taking machine shop two hours each day. I worked after school and Saturdays at a woodworking shop. Earning a little income improved my attitude about life somewhat; I was able to help buy things my sister and I needed for graduation including our class rings, pictures, and albums.

CHAPTER 7

LIFE GOES ON

The summer after I graduated from high school was an uncertain time for me. I worked at the wood shop. Mom was not doing well. The rheumatic fever she had suffered as a child left her with a damaged heart valve. The doctor was not able to control her blood pressure. She passed away in the hospital early in 1966.

I had received my draft notice. I had reservations about going into the army. The Vietnam war was raging; our boys were dying right and left. Therefore, I called on the navy recruiter; I wanted to join the navy though I would serve four years there rather than two in the army. I requested that I be allowed to continue my mechanical training, and the navy agreed; I joined and spent four years onboard a supertanker that refueled ships at sea under the cover of darkness.

We had two Mediterranean cruises during which we visited all the countries there. It was a very enjoyable time for me.

Before leaving on the first Mediterranean cruise, I went to a pawnshop in Jacksonville, Florida, our homeport, and bought a small sewing machine. Aboard ship, I developed a steady clientele of sailors who needed their clothes mended, patches sewn on, or their bell-bottom dungarees or uniform pants tailored to fit. The sailors liked the more stylish tapered shirts, jumpers, bell-bottoms, and pants. I made sure their clothes were much more appealing than were their standard-issue garments, and I charged them less than a stateside tailor would have.

I would ask them to bring me their well-fitting jeans, and I would lay them over their standard-issue uniform trousers and mark them where to taper the fit. I was very successful at that; by the time I was discharged, I had earned over $1,000 to go home with not counting many items I bought overseas such as tailored suits, recording equipment, and a clock.

The first year I was back, I tried to get my former employer to take me back on, but that did not happen, so the money I had saved came in handy. He hired me a year later, and I stayed for a few months. Then I met a woman at my best friend's wedding. The next year, I moved to Charlottesville, Virginia, got married, and took a job. We rented for one year before we were able to buy a house on the GI Bill; we lived in that place for twenty years. Over that time, that house doubled in value five times. We bought another home my wife liked, and we lived there for another twenty years, but it barely doubled in value.

My wife passed away in 1995. I sold the house recently because it was too big; I had to downsize. I now live in a small house in Scottsville, Virginia, about eighteen miles from Charlottesville. I also own a home in Oak Hill, where I vacation from time to time mainly on Labor Day and times I go for high school reunions. I still have two brothers and a sister living in Oak Hill, and I have numerous other Bibb family members including several nieces and nephews, cousins, and two sisters; one lives out of state and the other in Parkersburg, West Virginia. Dad had remarried and moved from where we lived before I came home again. The last old house we lived in burned down. The other house Dad rented out now belongs to my oldest brother, who still lives there.

I lost a good number of items I had made as well as woodworking equipment when Dad moved, but he did save most of the projects I made in high school shop. Among them were a wood lathe, metal vises, and an aluminum Lazy Susan I had made for Mom.

One of Mom's heirlooms was a porcelain coffee pot she kept in the dining room china cabinet; it was a gift to her from Dad after the birth of their third daughter. I wrote a poem about it.

Mother's Old Porcelain Coffee Pot

Mother's Old Porcelain Coffee Pot
There's not much left to treasure
from our mega home,
Most things we may have
cherished are now gone.
Not many things of value
resided in our family home.
Only one thing remains today
we can reflect upon.

I remember it sitting in the old china
closet where Mother kept it there.
Where it stayed most of our childhood,
And handled with the best of care.
A gift to Mother from Dad you see,
Upon the birth of their
third daughter to be.
It was given to her before
Mother passed away.
It sits in her home now where it will stay.
Seventy years ago a part of
our home it would play,
A family heirloom is still here today.

The last career move I made was to a job as an assistant refrigerator and air-conditioning mechanic. The job involved maintaining equipment including washing and cleaning it. I did that for several years until I began a preventive-maintenance program for the company; I started doing preventive maintenance on window air-conditioning units. Not long after that, I was asked to inventory all of a medical center's equipment in ninety-nine buildings; they wanted to make sure all their equipment would be in good repair. The medical center had to comply with regulations concerning equipment maintenance or possibly lose its accreditation.

After I entered all the data, I found myself as the author of three-inch-thick volumes of equipment records. A contract came to enter all data into a new PM system. The contractor printed out work orders for PM for a year or so. Next thing I knew, I received a computer and was told I would be responsible for printing out the weekly PM schedules and entering new equipment data updates. This system performed well. Next thing I knew, we were on the internet and updating data online.

That was only one aspect of my job description. I agreed to accept a position as a supervisor, but I later came to regret that. As soon as this happened, the night shift worker employees of the Zone 2 Maintenance crew with the stock RM. I became the purchasing agent for the company as well. I became the supervisor of approximately twenty employees overnight. I worked at that job for thirty-two years.

Just before I was about to retire, they asked me to be a project manager in addition to my other numerous responsibilities. I asked for more money, but they said there would be none. I let them know I would be retiring soon. After I retired, they asked me to work part time as they had no one to do the job, and I did that for a year and a half until they told me my services were no longer required. I went home—the end of my career.

Working in coal mines was dangerous, but so was working with air-conditioning equipment considering all the air circulating through outpatient rooms, operating rooms, morgues, and so on. I have probably been exposed to all that as well as asbestos insulation in the mechanical rooms in those ninety-nine buildings we maintained.

I recall going on a bus tour with my wife some years ago. We toured all the sites of the rich and famous. We rode most all day and stopped at hotels at night. There was no limit to the food we enjoyed. One stop was at a seafood market where everyone picked out the seafood for the evening dinner later that day. We were living large.

We visiting several mansions that had been owned by the coal magnates of the day on the East Coast including one belonging to the Berwind family, who had owned the Minden coal mine. The Burwind mansion reminded me very much of the magnificent structures I had seen in Italy, Spain, and Greece while I was on my two Mediterranean cruises in the navy. The rooms had gigantic, tall ceilings and paintings by Italian artists. I saw humungous pieces of furniture everywhere. I saw gold-plated faucets and white marble everywhere. Everything had been imported from Italy along with painters, carpenters, and stonemasons. The large carpets on all the floors had come from India.

We learned that the home was heated and cooled year-round whether occupied or not. There were large air-conditioning units and large coal furnaces with an eight-month supply of coal—eight tons—on hand at all times for the boilers. Upon seeing all this, I began to wonder why these mine owners deserved such a life. When comparing all this to the meager life of coal miners, I felt nauseous. I cannot complain about the lifestyle I have attained; middle class was not too bad in years past, but now, there is no middle class. I guess we did not know how good we had had it.

When you compare all that wealth to the $2 scrip books we had to spend in the company store, you might think that though miners were not slaves, they were close to that.

CHAPTER 8

HINDSIGHT IS 20/20

As I wrote this book, I came to realize that the world beyond coal-mining towns was not that different from conditions miners suffered underground. Conditions underground were different from those above ground, but workers in both places have to deal with mistreatment, unhealthy working conditions, and hazards; the differences were not that great; we had jobs to do rain or shine, wet or cold.

The $1.95 an hour wage in the mines beat the 85¢ an hour I earned working in the wood shop and the $1.33 an hour I earned at the machine shop for one and a half years. I stood under a four-foot-square air-conditioning vent eight hours a day until my head was spinning, my nose was running, and my sinuses were clogged by the rushing air and the abrasive dust from the grinding wheel. I did not have a mask or other health-related safety equipment. Start to see what I'm saying? And I worked in the hospital for thirty-five years and was exposed to health-related hazards. (As I have indicated, a safety program has been put into place.)

But the same attitudes prevailed. Management at any level was always nice about receiving any complaints, but it did not prevent exposure to hazardous material and the health-related issues some employees developed. Something to see is six men trying to move a 150-HP, cast-iron motor down six flights of stairs by hand. No equipment—just bare hands and mashed toes. It probably weighed 600 pounds. Where to stand was always a question. Have you ever carried anything like that downstairs? There was not room enough to stand on any stair.

We were constantly maintaining chemicals to treat all water systems. The air conditioner chill water systems condensed the water systems' fan cooling of machinery from cooling towers. One worker got his boots wet inside with one of these chemicals, and he shed all the skin on the bottom of his feet, and that caused him to go on disability. He was just a fellow West Virginian trying to feed his family. I could go on and on, but we did have good health insurance and a good retirement plan. That was worth staying for if nothing else. I can say I am very grateful for it today.

However, as the old saying goes, one hand washes the other. I guess we could have had it much worse than workers in some other countries did, where they might cut off one hand to teach you a lesson. Do as I say or else! I guess you would be lucky. Some places would cut off your head. Therefore, I guess the labor force will have to continue to beat the drum slowly if it wants to survive. Do not make too much noise—someone might hear you. That old song about a miner's soul and the company's store still rings true today, and miners could have lost their bodies as well as their souls in the mines. Many miners did—God rest their souls.

Things gradually got better at work. We received grants to start a project to abate all asbestos from all building there. When I started there in 1970, the new medical education building was under construction across the street from the hospital, and they were spraying asbestos into it. When I left there in 2005, all the buildings had had all asbestos abated—what a waste, what an expense. Paying taxes in this area paid for it all. Put it in take it out. Except for all of us who suffered; many died from the exposure. Of course, all that really mattered was the tremendous salaries those at the top made. Even doctors would create their own departments and businesses and charge high prices for their services to support their grand lifestyles. Their goal was to break away from state control and the state itself so they could control their own destinies. They no longer complied with many rules, and they had complete control over their salaries—blackmail you might say at the expense of the insurance companies and the hospitals I am sure. Greed is everywhere!

I never felt I needed much money; I was never bothered about not having much. I was happy and grateful for what we had. We managed until better times came along, but even then, I did not set the world on fire and become rich. The wages I earned when I started working were low, but over the years, my salary grew to above a middle-income level. In the meantime, my wife and I had all we needed to survive; we were able to own a home and raise a child.

Since the beginning of time, humans have been greedy—one bite of forbidden fruit sent humankind out to a laborious life in this world. God, who had made good, loving people, saw this same greed in others and wiped them out in a flood; he started over with just Noah and his family. But as history will tell you, it happened again and again, and here we are, y'all.

Greedy sharks are still out there trying to lend you money, reverse your mortgage, or sell you overpriced insurance, vinyl siding for your house, or miracle cures, and they tell you you'll have to act immediately. The ones I fear the most are those who want to put people in nursing homes. "Call now!" they say, and they repeat their phone numbers seventeen times per commercial.

One Minden resident lived in a large company house. He was always paying miners cash for their scrip books, which allowed them to shop other places besides the company store. Any way you look at it, I'm sure the miners ended up on the losing end of those transactions due to that man's greed. Any way they could find to outdo the poor coal miners, they did, and then they would blame that on the miners. Miners owed their souls to the company store and to everyone else.

CHAPTER 9

PET PEEVES

When I came to Charlottesville, Virginia, in 1970, I found a small town full of friendly people. The area was thriving very well and growing slowly. Today, it has gone the other way. Yes, it has grown, especially on North 29 and into the next two counties along Route 29. We should be next-door neighbors with Fairfax, Virginia, any day now.

When I came home, I rented an upstairs apartment for $100 a month. After we were married, we rented a basement apartment for $100 a month for a year. We bought a three-bedroom house for $20,000 in 1970. By 1990, it had doubled in value five times, but that second home, as I mentioned, did not appreciate anywhere near as much by the time I sold it in 2018 due to greed and dirt-poor pay.

Before we were married, my wife worked as a receptionist for two well-known surgeons for eight years. She never earned much, and I do not know if she received any benefits. Though she wasn't treated well by most of the staff, she received nice gifts at Christmas, but don't think we could eat them! Usually, they were gifts that came from some faraway places others were able to go. She frequently had to fill in for most everyone else. When the nurses were not there, she had to perform nursing duties.

One day after work, I told her to tell them she was quitting with no notice. One Friday evening, I met her walking home; at the time, she was living with her parents. She had quit, and we joyously walked home. She had a longtime friend at the hospital who got her a job working there—better pay, better atmosphere, better benefits, and insurance and retirement—better everything. She worked there for thirty-two years before she retired.

Unfortunately, in 1984, she discovered a depression on the skin on her chest. The diagnosis was cancer. After surgery, she didn't undergo any treatment; the node had been small and hadn't spread. She did very well after that for nearly twenty years. In 2002, however, it had started to spread to her bones and soft tissue. Six years of chemo went by, and the treatment became worse than the cure. Therefore, she decided she had had enough. She passed away five months later in 2005. I remember one of our past president's ways of expressing troubling situations; he said, "It is what it is." I'll give you one guess who that was.

Well, I don't like to see people fail when they put effort into something, but I haven't seen anyone I know or have been around who did amazingly well by doing honest, hard work. Of course, people could win the lottery, but I don't know anyone who has. I thought I would try it one time and bought $20 of scratch-off tickets. I scratched and scratched and won $20. I put that in my pocket and have never tried it again.

Enough about greed and people putting their feet on other people's hands as they reach for a higher rung on the ladder on their way to a better life. As they say down home in the South, "Shut your mouth before you say something you'll always regret." I say amen to that.

CHAPTER 10

WHERE'S THAT COAL BUCKET?

The old, warm, coal heater we warmed our house with would go out at times before morning. Dad would build a fire and get it burning very good before bedtime. Then he would cover the entire fire with what we called slack—very fine coal dust. Slack was created when coal was dug out and small granules would fall to the way side below in fire piles. The slack would smother the flames down to the point that it would create a large lump of charcoal. That usually kept the house warm all night. But at times, it would burn up if the flames broke through the big lump, and it would then burn quickly. That meant the house would be very cold the next morning.

Dad would get coal any way he could from any surplus that might be available from the mine. Many times, he would pick up coal that fell off coal cars along the tracks. According to my brothers, when they were young, Dad would drop them off at the tracks with large buckets they had to fill with small lumps of coal, and that could take them the whole day. Later, when we had that coal mine, we had all we needed for some time.

When I was three or four, I'd get into the coalhouse to play, and I would end up very dirty; that's what our good neighbors told me repeatedly over the years. The coal company built two-sided coalhouses of cement on brick at the houses of their miners. These were four- to five-foot buildings with small doors on each end—one to put coal in and the other to retrieve it. The coal company delivered the coal to the miners and took the cost out of their pay as they did for other services the company provided them. Miners owed everything to the coal companies.

The houses owned by the coal companies usually had one or two fireplaces. The people renting them had to put in pipes to vent the kitchen stoves. There was usually a chimney connection in the kitchen for a coal-fired range to cook and bake on.

Most of the coal mined for industry back in the day was lump coal; the fine stuff fell to the wayside until a use for it was found—it could create hotter fires that could melt steel and so on. But that meant the production of much finer coal, and such pulverized coal would float in the air and be breathed in by the miners not intentionally of course. An additional danger was that such fine coal was very volatile; it could combust and cause great explosions underground. Bet that would wake you up if your mind was wandering. With all the loud noise of the machinery rattling and clanking, you probably were not very coherent at that time.

Sometimes when we had a good fire going in the fireplace, we would poke the coals, and some would fall off all of a sudden and flare up; red-hot coals would pop out onto the wood or linoleum floor. Someone would jump up, grab a shovel, and put the coals back on the grate to keep them from burning the house down. But that didn't stop some homes from burning down due to chimney fires.

CHAPTER 11

MAKING DO

When the miners went on strike or when a mine was shutting down, the union would make surplus food available to eligible miners. I remember taking either a wagon or a sled if there was snow, and up the railroad tracks we would go walking, running, laughing, and playing all the way to the schoolhouse that was also the union hall at the upper end near the first bridge.

The people passing out federal government surplus food for the miners were volunteer residents of Minden. We received large boxes of American cheese—about five pounds each—and cans of meat. Sometimes, it was actually canned beef, like roast beef, but in later years, it was something like Spam nonetheless in good-sized cans. We received powered milk, but that wasn't easy to reconstitute, and it had an off taste. There were also cans of peanut butter, pounds of butter, dehydrated powered eggs, and bags of rice. These items supplemented the vegetables and fruits we had canned in the fall, and at times, we had hundreds of jars of that. Usually by spring, our family of ten would have used up most of our canned food. Some of the jars would freeze in cold temperatures.

In the later days, on one of our young adventures in the coal camp, we came upon a weed-covered wooden building. It had apparently been a sort of firehouse that a volunteer fire brigade used. It had a metal fire hose reel with a two-and-a-half-inch cotton fire hose. There were fire hydrants throughout Minden. These connected to a fire hose for the brigade to wet down a burning structure. It was a hand-pulled rig with large metal spoke wheels on each side and a handle to pull it to the fire; that took at least two men.

There had been a number of such fire stations in Minden, but this one seemed to be the last. We were very interested in it. We asked the company real estate agent if we could have the hose reel since it had been abandoned for years. He agreed, and we set out to remove it from the partially dilapidated building. That was not easy, but we pulled it home. Dad removed the metal and wooden wheels and mounted them in the front yard of the last house we lived in. He painted them red and white. They looked very nice along the front of the house. We would put Christmas lights on them at that time of year, and I remember sleigh riding between them many years. It is amazing how much history and memories can be brought out into the present day.

Holes began to appear under one house we lived in due to mining activity in the area. When they got bigger, Mom said that was enough; she told us to pack up because we were moving, and we did. The company had compensated us when a large hole caved in far up on the property, but holes that close to the house made Mom frightened for our lives. The old mining timbers were beginning to rot and decay, and old Minden shafts were caving in due to that.

CHAPTER 12

SURVIVING THE RAINS

The coal camp experienced many flash floods whenever Arbuckle Creek breached its banks. One big flash flood came because of a lot of rain. Apparently, water from all the rain had built up on top of the slate dump, which was near the first few houses at the bottom of Minden Hill. Two houses were flooded with a tremendous amount of water and red dog and burnt slate from the slate dump. The rooms filled to the roofs inside with red dog. They tore those houses down, and later, other homes became vacant and burned down over the years.

Apparently, the coal company still owned the land the houses had sat on. Over the years, the land rights were sold to a rafting company. Then, more of the last houses began to burn down, and some were occupied at the time. Today, very few houses remain there.

A lot has happened to the mining town. Industries set up businesses there, but they did not stay long. Much manufacturing residue contaminated the soil; PCBs and failing sewer plant waste presented hazardous living conditions throughout Minden. Many claims of cases of cancer were reported in the community, and a great deal of effort went into testing and cleaning up the area.

A new sewer system was installed, but the complaints became louder, so that stopped. The city of Oak Hill annexed the town as a subdivision, and that created more cause for complaints and further efforts to clean and process the soil in affected areas, and the sewer-system installation resumed.

The creek continues to flood from time to time, but due to many efforts of the Minden Community Center, the rafting company, and others, people still live there—at last count, about two hundred. As you can imagine, much of the pollution was due to greed and the desire for profit.

CHAPTER 13

DETERMINATION
AND COMPASSION

You know kids—they love to find excitement of any kind, and their attention spans aren't long even in a coal-mining town that was mostly just country and coal. I used to love to draw and color as a kid. I would get the funny papers, pick out some of the cartoon characters, and draw them just by looking at them, not by tracing them.

I was always interested in log cabins. When I was young, a friend and I played with a Lincoln Logs set he had. That was due to my interest in TV Westerns, which always showed great-looking log cabins. We would build cabins out of anything we could, and that interest has stayed with me even to this day. I am amazed at the modern log structures being built today.

About twenty years ago, I bought some property near Fort Union and built something that resembled a log cabin, though it was small—one room with a loft on a site down a hill and above a creek. I built it using standard construction techniques, and I sided it with log siding. Today, I'm older, and it's an effort to keep up with it. I nonetheless enjoy sitting on the porch swing and listening to the water flowing in the creek even though I get there usually just to keep the trees cut back and the grass mowed. I went to the property yesterday, rode the mower for six hours, and could barely get out of the truck at home. I thought that selling my home in Charlottesville would allow me to build a nice one there, but that proved futile. I needed to downsize, so I moved to a smaller home.

I feel compassion for miners who have to work many hard years before they can retire and enjoy what remains of their lives. I can't imagine any young man wanting to be a miner today. He would have to have no alternatives, no other possibilities. I hope that any miners today can escape the greed and abuse the miners of my day had to suffer in Minden, West Virginia, as they simply tried to provide for their families.

Years after I left Minden, my memories of growing up there prompted me to write this book about the abuses miners had to suffer. If they had only received a fair wage, they would have been able to live better lives for themselves and provide for their children and grandchildren. Coal companies provided for their miners to some degree, but they charged for every service they provided. The miners and their families had to pinch every penny to have something near a basic life.

I have heard stories about miners in the first days who had to work in tunnels just eighteen inches to two feet high; they would do so by lying on their backs and wielding picks to cut coal. Then, they would have to get that coal loaded in carts and get it out of the mine to get credit for their labor. Some miners had their family members pull their carts out and back in so they could keep working with their picks. At times, other miners stole the credit for coal they hadn't mined. Can you imagine the disappointment and loss of labor and pay? In the early days of mining, there were few if any laws to protect common laborers. They were little better than slaves working in horrible conditions.

The open flames on their hats were the only light they could work by, but those fires could ignite the methane gas that could build up in the mines. They also had to contend with large rats that made their homes in the mines; those rats would steal miners' lunches if they could. The invention of the metal lunch box was very much welcome by those who could afford to buy them.

And working in wet clothes all day from lying on the ground did not prove to be very healthy circumstances for miners particularly when the temperature would be around fifty degrees year-round and water would drip on them constantly. Such deep, dark, damp conditions combined with coal dust shortened their lives of near slavery.

Many people still suffer lives of slavery—think about the homeless, the downtrodden, the unemployed waiting in endless lines for food and drug addicts who are slaves to their cravings. The slavery in their lives has totally freed them of all responsibility you might say. The greed of the few forced these conditions on the many, and that will probably always be the case. Unless you have lived under some of these conditions, you might not be grateful for what you have.

The coal abundant in the southern area of West Virginia is bituminous coal, a soft coal that burns well and gives off minimal amount of pollutants. It is very good for producing coke, which is needed to produce high heat for metal smelting. The coal in this region was called high coal; some seams were six feet deep, and that made mining easier and it made miners more productive, but the profits went to the owners of the mines, not the miners, who received little. The area bears names indicating coal was king, and some towns had names similar to "High Coal."

The old Baptist church in Minden was originally the home of Captain Thurmond. It is the second church beyond the old company store farther down the road and beyond the railroad crossing and trestle. The captain built this house after the Civil War. The foundation has large rock blocks that came from Pea Ridge, near Oak Hill. The Union Army burned and destroyed it all except for the rock foundation. It still remains Minden Baptist Church and is in service to this day.

There are still three churches in service. The Methodist church, which is now the Minden Community Center, is also still used as a worshipping church. The last one is in Rock Lick, which also is a functioning church. The congregations of these churches function as a committed operation to maintain their livelihood. Their congregations are small, but all the members know each other well. They support one another, which is rare in this day. They continue to serve our Lord.

CHAPTER 14

WHAT'S IMPORTANT?

I hope this book will draw attention to how some have found ways to use their positions to gain favors in life. I don't mean to condemn them; I just want to make it clear how they achieved what they have achieved. Many people have dreams about becoming rich quickly, and they don't care about how they do that. And some people have passed that attitude onto their children consciously or subconsciously. They want their children to have everything they never had, but some of them end up educated but living in basements waiting for the next high. The evidence is on the streets everywhere—homeless people and drug users' needles.

We have lost our way. What is important? The pressures of life have forced us to become an out-of-control world populated by zombies. Most people in this world are under stress and are killing those they think are standing in their way, and they leave death and dysfunction in their wake.

What will teach us to correct our errors? Will refugees continue to risk their lives on rubber rafts to find new worlds and new lives? There will be more three-year-olds who wash up on beaches separated from their families if they survive.

They cannot all come to this country. If they do, they will create the same conditions here that they suffered in their countries of origin. Drug cartels promote this lifestyle for many without concern for any others, and this has turned our youth into zombies who care for nothing. Some youth today have no respect for law. If we lose them all, no one will be safe. Can you imagine the living conditions of everyone taking that route? We could very well be on the verge of this today. So what is our plight if we want to make changes? Is there any wonder why we owe our souls to that ol' company store?

Printed in the United States
By Bookmasters